Understanding feminism

Find out everything you need to know about feminism, its origins and its various forms in a clear and compact format

Lena Hafermann

CONTENTS

What you can expect in this book

MeToo movement, gender pay gap, manspreading, catcalling - you hear these terms more and more often these days, and they all revolve around one topic: feminism. Feminism affects us all and a sound basic knowledge of the subject is essential, especially now. In this book, you will learn what all these terms mean and how they relate to feminism. But what exactly is feminism? Haven't we all had equal rights for a long time? In principle

Feminism for equal rights and equal opportunities regardless of gender. In countries such as Pakistan,

Chad or Iran, women are still treated like second-class people without rights. Many are forced into marriage, are not allowed to go to school or work and are only allowed to leave the house veiled and accompanied by their husbands.

In Germany, the situation is more advanced, but the oppression of women was not that long ago - women were not allowed to vote until 1919, they were not allowed to open their own bank account until 1958, they had to obey their husbands and women were still legally obliged to run the household until 1977. A lot has changed since then; according to Article 3 of the Basic Law, men and women are equal before the law. In reality, however, traces of patriarchy can still be seen:

There is unequal pay in the labour market, women still do most of the housework, have a harder time at work as they are perceived as less qualified than male colleagues, they are shown less respect, the female body is sexualized and products such as drugs and cars are tailored to the male body. In addition, one in three women experience sexual violence, which has little or no consequences and is committed by men in 98% of all cases. This is only a fraction of all the areas in which women are disadvantaged. Feminism highlights and opposes all of this unequal treatment.

But is there "the" one feminism? In which areas is feminism necessary? Does feminism also help men? And what can I do for feminism? These questions are answered in this book. Once you understand how sexism works, how it manifests itself and how feminism can help combat it, you too can contribute to creating a modern world without gender discrimination.

Understanding feminism

WHAT IS FEMINISM?

First of all, we need to understand what feminism actually is. The term first appeared in 1837, when the French social critic Charles Fourier used the word "féminisme" to describe the self-determination of women.

The German word Feminismus has its origins here and is derived from the Latin word femina, which means woman. It is defined in the Duden dictionary as a "direction of the women's movement that, based on the needs of women, strives for a fundamental change in social norms (for example, the traditional distribution of roles) and patriarchal culture." However, as this term is so diverse and constantly changing over the years, there is no single correct definition. The American literary scholar Bell Hooks describes feminism somewhat more politically as "a movement that seeks to abolish sexism, sexist exploitation and oppression."

The famous British actress and UN Special Envoy Emma Watson explains: "Feminism is about giving women a choice. Feminism is not a stick to beat other women with. It's about freedom, liberation and self-determination. If you are for equality, you are a feminist." And Nigerian writer Chimamanda Ngozi Adichie calls anyone who "believes in the social, political and economic equality of the sexes" a feminist. At least all these definitions have something in common: feminism strives for freedom, self-determination, equal rights and equal opportunities regardless of gender.

It is directed against a patriarchal, sexist system that has prevailed for thousands of years and is responsible for the ongoing oppression and discrimination of women, because in patriarchy, women are subordinate to men and must abide by their decisions . Such cultural views are criticized by feminism. However, feminism does not want to bring women to power while oppressing men; this social order is called matriarchy. Feminism also has nothing to do with hatred of men;

the term for this is misandry. It merely contradicts the dominant patriarchal norms. Ultimately, the aim is to create a fair society for all in which no gender is disadvantaged or favored.

DOES "THE" FEMINISM EXIST?

As we have already established, feminism is diverse. Depending on the current, a different understanding of gender, society and inequality is represented. There are therefore different currents, some of which I would like to briefly introduce to you below.

Liberal feminism is committed to gender-independent equality. Everyone should be able to develop freely according to their own talents and ideas, without being prevented from doing so because of their gender, origin or sexuality. Clichés should be broken so that women are no longer forced into the role of housewife and men are no longer forced into the role of sole breadwinner, and the focus is on equal opportunities. Everyone should be able to express themselves individually.

Differentiating feminism emphasizes the differences between the sexes. This is derived from biological differences and differences between the sexes that have arisen due to culture and society. Its proponents argue that women, as potential mothers, are generally more empathetic, helpful and social than men, meaning that they need to be more involved in important areas such as global politics and the economy. There should be less focus on male standards and at the same time typically female characteristics should be promoted in order to enable peaceful coexistence worldwide.

Conservative feminism is similar to the current of differentiating feminism in that it emphasizes gender differences. Nevertheless, women should not only have to be housewives and mothers, but should also have equal opportunities in professional life, business and politics. The representatives justify this with the female skills that can offer considerable advantages. Traditional values should be preserved.

Socialist feminism emphasizes the equality of the sexes. It sees capitalism and patriarchy as the cause of structural discrimination and wants to strengthen the role of women in society in order to overcome the capitalist system. After all, it is mostly women who perform unpaid care work or reproductive work in the form of providing for people.

Ecological feminism disapproves of the links between the exploitation of nature and the oppression of women. After all, there are similarities between the reproductive capacity of nature and that of women, and environmental degradation particularly affects women as mothers and often farmers in the Third World. Therefore, feminist theories must include an ecological perspective, while the solution to environmental problems should include a feminist perspective.

Radical feminism calls for a revolution to overcome patriarchy, as men have been controlling and oppressing at all levels for ages. Therefore, according to its representatives, not only male privileges, but all gender differences should be eliminated. The mere advancement of women is not enough.

Queer feminism opposes the entire system that divides people into genders. It understands gender as something that is assigned to you by society and not as something biologically or psychologically predetermined. He stands up for all those who are discriminated against in any way, including transgender, dark-skinned, lesbian or poor women. Its aim is to dissolve gender in order to overcome discrimination.

GOALS OF FEMINISM

You can see from the various feminist movements that there are no uniformly formulated goals. After all, some movements contradict each other. At the very least, they all call for equal rights, self-determination, freedom and equal opportunities, regardless of gender, and campaign against discrimination. The recognition of and respect for women's human dignity are paramount. Acts of violence against women should not be tolerated simply because they are seen as the supposedly weaker sex. The behavior of women should not be judged differently from that of men simply because they are women. Women should be treated with the same respect as men.

The aim is to break through stereotypical role models in order to combat the different treatment of the sexes. Women should not only see themselves as mothers and housewives, but should also be able to live out their careers like men. Men should also be accepted as househusbands and fathers without being stigmatized. Women should be able to come to power just as easily as men so that they too can influence society.

Sexuality should be able to be lived out freely. In principle, no one should be disadvantaged in any area simply because of their gender. After all, men can also be disadvantaged, which feminism also takes into account. Ultimately, the aim is to achieve a fair society for all.

THE HISTORY OF FEMINISM

Beginnings

Feminism and the prevailing views on it are constantly changing. Different demands are made depending on the era, society and cultural milieu. The beginnings of feminism in Germany began at the end of the 18th century during the French Revolution, when men from lower classes fought for political and social rights. Constitutions with catalogs of basic rights were passed, but these were only granted to women to a limited extent. Bourgeois women took this as an opportunity to fight for their own rights.

The focus was on the right to education, better working conditions and equality between men and women. Until then, women had always been under the rule of their husbands and had to submit to their decisions. After the revolution, however, women were prohibited from being politically active or forming associations, and famous women's rights activists such as Olympe de Gouges were executed.

First wave

The first wave of feminism emerged in the mid-19th century in many European countries, the USA and Australia. In Great Britain, the Contagious Diseases Acts, which made prostitution state-controlled and considered women solely responsible for the spread of venereal diseases, were enforced from 1869.

The first General German Women's Association was founded with the aim of improving educational opportunities for women and enabling them to pursue a profession. To this end, industrial and commercial schools specifically for women, equal pay for equal work and equality between men and women were demanded. From 1896, women were admitted to university for the first time. This also led to the creation of new courses of study, such as social work.

The Women's Social and Political Union was founded in England. The members, known as suffragettes, protested for women's suffrage through hunger strikes, disruption of public events and parliamentary boycotts. This gave rise to feminist awareness, which spread to other countries. As a result of years of protests, voting rights for women aged 21 and over were included in the Weimar Constitution in Germany in 1919. Apart from Finland, Germany was the first

European country in which women were allowed to vote. This was also the first time they were allowed to participate in political power. At the same time, paternal guardianship over unmarried women of legal age and the guardianship of the husband were abolished.

During the First World War, the initial successes of the feminist movements slowed down. While the men fought as soldiers at the front, the women had to work in factories. Even after the war, when a large proportion of the men were either seriously wounded or dead, women had to provide for the family's income and take care of the household at the same time. The war and German inflation from 1914 to 1923 caused social hardship among war orphans and war widows, which led to food riots and mass strikes by women workers. In the course of the global economic crisis in 1929, many jobs were lost, which particularly affected women. As a result, they often had to take on the traditional role of housewife and mother again.

When the National Socialists came to power in 1933, the first wave of feminism came to an end. Women's associations and organizations were dissolved or brought into line, women were banned from working in higher professions and their right to vote was revoked. Famous women's rights activists and opponents of the Nazi regime such as Anita Augspurg and Alice Salomon had to flee into exile.

In addition, the Nazis spread an enemy image of intellectual, self-determined women. The true female destiny was to be a housewife and mother. This re-established traditional gender relations. After the Second World War and the fall of the Nazi regime, women once again had to work to support their families when their husbands were wounded or deceased. As Germany gradually recovered in the 1950s, men were once again the sole breadwinners in the family, while women returned to being housewives and mothers. However, this did not last long.

Second wave

Feminism was revived from the 1960s onwards. The famous "tomato throw" of 1969 ushered in the second wave of feminism. The spokesperson for the Action Council for the Liberation of Women, Helke Sander, accused the SDS men of ignoring the discrimination against women without being heeded by them.

Sigrid Rüder then threw tomatoes in the direction of the board table. On the same day, women's groups formed to take action against unequal treatment. Women were hardly represented at secondary schools and universities, only one in three women was in employment and they had hardly any participation in politics. The women who were employed only worked in gender-typical jobs such as secretary or teacher and were poorly paid.

In addition, women were not allowed to open their own bank accounts or dispose of their assets until 1962, until 1977 they needed their husband's permission to pursue a profession and in the event of divorce, the woman was generally regarded as the guilty party and not supported financially. Abortions were prohibited, women could not take legal action against marital rape and they were solely responsible for the household.

The feminist Simone de Beauvoir published the book "The Opposite Sex", in which she dispelled myths about women, highlighted the differences between biological and social gender and made it clear that women are forced into the role of housewife and are not meant to be. The book made waves and women's movements once again campaigned for women's independence and self-determination and drew attention to the disadvantages they faced. In particular, they fought against lower pay, rigid role models, restricted access to education and the ban on abortions.

From 1957 onwards, the legal provisions that violated Article 3 of the Basic Law as a requirement of equal rights were gradually abolished in the FRG. From 1994, the addition was added to Article 3: "The state shall promote the actual implementation of equal rights for women and men and shall work towards the elimination of existing disadvantages." In 1961, a woman became Federal Minister for the first time. It was Elisabeth Schwarzhaupt, who was responsible for healthcare.

From the 1980s onwards, the Greens experienced an upswing as they wanted to promote feminism. The CDU also reformed its policies and campaigned for a better work-life balance. Many prominent women admitted to having an abortion despite the poor hygiene standards and the ban. As a result of the second wave, abortions were permitted under certain conditions, education was provided on sexuality and sexual offenses, women could decide for themselves whether and as what they wanted to work, and women's quotas and childcare quotas were introduced to make it easier for women to work.

In 1977, the "housewife marriage" law was abolished, meaning that the woman was no longer legally obliged to run the household. The principle of fault in divorce was withdrawn and the woman's surname could also be adopted as the family name. Following this reform of family law, there were also modernizations in teaching and research: for the first time in 1976, there was a programme for women at the Free University in Berlin, which dealt with women in history, politics, culture and the sciences. Gender studies were introduced in 1997 to investigate gender relations. Furthermore, a law on equal treatment of men and women in the workplace was passed in 1980, which, in addition to equal treatment, stipulated equal pay for equal work regardless of gender.

Third wave

The third wave of feminism began in the mid-1990s. The term emerged from the American "Third Wave Feminism" and focuses on the diversity of female identities and experiences. Heterosexuality as a social norm and the binary gender order have been questioned ever since.

Intersectional feminism developed, which points to the possibility of multiple discrimination. After all, there is also racism (discrimination based on origin), ableism (discrimination against people with disabilities) and classism (discrimination based on social origin). What it means to be a woman or a man is not fixed and is constantly changing. In the course of the third wave, marriage between people of the same sex was permitted, among other things.

Since the UN World Conference on Women in Beijing in 1995, measures have been established to achieve gender equality and the realization of women's rights. In particular, these include poverty, education, violence against women, women in professional life and in positions of power, human rights, the environment, media and childhood. The focus is on self-confidence, freedom, self-determination and gender equality.

At the same time, anti-feminism is on the rise; many men want to retain their privileges and ignore or defame feminism accordingly. Nevertheless, everyday sexism and discrimination are increasingly being talked about publicly in order to highlight and minimize the patriarchal structures that still prevail.

WHY IS FEMINISM IMPORTANT?

Since feminism has been around for so long, you would think we would have achieved gender equality long ago. Women can vote, have a job, sexual assault is forbidden. At least that's the theory. In the USA, however, around four million people took to the streets for the Women's March on January 21, 2017. In Spain, 5.3 million people protested in strikes in 2018. In Germany, too, not everyone is satisfied with the current situation.

Gender equality is desirable in both legal and social terms, but in practice it is still a long way off. Below you can see the areas in which feminism is still far from achieving its goal.

According to the Federal Ministry for Family Affairs, Senior Citizens, Women and Youth, women spend an average of 52.4% more time per day on unpaid care work than men. This includes all household work, gardening, caring for and looking after children and adults, unpaid help for other households and voluntary work. Travel times were also taken into account.

Men do around two hours and 46 minutes of this work per day, women around four hours and 13 minutes. Even if women earn the main income in the family, they usually work more in the household. This gender care gap illustrates the different amount of time spent on so-called care work. And it is not without consequences: Women are significantly more likely to work part-time than men in order to manage unpaid care work. This also has an impact on their lower income and pension. The difference is particularly extreme among 34-year-olds:

Women spend 110.6% more of their time on unpaid tasks than men. It is precisely at this age that key life decisions are made and the amount of time spent on children increases. Most of the care work is done in households with children in particular, as childcare takes up a lot of time. In addition, women often take on the more intimate, strenuous and emotionally stressful tasks when it comes to caring for their parents, for example. In the UK, for example, women provide 70% of unpaid care and receive even less support than men.

The UK Office for National Statistics found that women in the UK have around five hours less free time per week as a result and are even more likely to combine their remaining free time with household chores.

In Uganda, women even work six hours a day more than men. This discrepancy has significant consequences: it has a negative impact on women's health. According to a Canadian study from 2016, women have poorer outcomes after heart surgery as they immediately resume their unpaid work after the operation, while men rest and are cared for after an operation. In addition, women suffer stress, anxiety and depression at work twice as often as men. Women's health suffers more than men's, particularly in areas where a lot of overtime is worked; working between 41 and 55 hours per week has a negative effect on women, while there is no negative effect on men.

According to a Swedish study, the risk of developing heart disease and cancer triples if they work more than 60 hours a week for 30 years. However, this is not due to a fundamentally lower stress tolerance in women; they simply take on so much of the unpaid work that they are not capable of doing more at work. Instead, they keep their husbands' backs free by working at home and often work part-time, which puts less strain on him, but at the same time they earn less. Despite the physical and mental strain, care work is often not seen as real work. A fair division of care work between couples would lead to better opportunities on the labor market, higher incomes and higher independent pension entitlements for women.

Sexism starts with small things that sometimes go unnoticed in everyday life. You may have noticed that men in particular sit with their legs apart on the bus or train. This is not an isolated case, but occurs so frequently that there is an established term for it: Manspreading. Men spread their legs five times as often on the train as women and, contrary to popular belief, they don't do this for physical reasons, according to scientific findings.

They take the space because they subconsciously think they are entitled to it. The lack of consideration is the expression of a dominance and power behavior with which they subliminally want to make their place in the world clear. Even as children, they are taught that they are entitled to something that they should take. The desire to show presence is therefore already learned in childhood. After all, boys are always shown and trained to behave in an action-oriented and competitive manner.

Girls, on the other hand, learn early on to give way to others and to take a back seat. So while boys are expected and encouraged to behave loudly, confidently and dominantly, girls are punished for it. Boys are also encouraged not to question themselves when they receive attention in a negative way. Girls, on the other hand, should be able to control themselves and be considerate. What is learned so early in childhood does not suddenly change in adulthood. Nevertheless, this also occurs in women, albeit to a lesser extent.

However, they don't sit down with their legs apart, but by placing their bag or rucksack on the empty seat next to their seat. This is called shebagging. However, fewer people have a problem drawing a woman's attention to this; women are less likely to concede the extra space than a man. If you are ever confronted with manspreading or shebagging, you can either silently demand your place by spreading out as well, or you can speak to the man or woman about taking up too much space, but without asking or apologizing. After all, you are not misbehaving, you are entitled to the space and you can demand it. In addition, there are usually other people on the train or bus who can come to your aid in an emergency.

Another example of discrimination that is not immediately obvious: public toilets. You've probably noticed that there are always longer queues in front of women's toilets than men's at concerts or in cinemas. However, this is not primarily because women simply have to go to the toilet more often: There are simply more toilet facilities in men's restrooms. According to the Ordinance on Places of Assembly, eight toilets and twelve urinals must be available for 1000 men; for women, only twelve toilets. Although most toilets have the same floor space, the urinals mean that the square meters can be used by more people at the same time.

So it's no wonder that men's toilets go faster. In addition, normal toilet use takes longer for women than for men for anatomical reasons. In addition, most elderly and disabled people are female and therefore also take longer. Furthermore, a significant number of women of childbearing age have their period, which means that they still have to change their pad, tampon or menstrual cup. Not to mention the fact that women suffer from bladder infections eight times as often as men and therefore also need to go to the toilet more often. Due to these biological differences, the toilet distribution is anything but fair.

If we take a look at other countries, we notice an even more serious problem when it comes to toilets: 30% of all women do not have access to safe toilets. According to WaterAid, girls and women spend a total of 97 billion hours looking for a safe place to go to the toilet. In developing countries, many female workers even try to avoid going to the toilet all day for lack of a safe place to go and clean water. As a result, they don't drink during the day, which puts them at risk of dehydration, bladder and urinary tract infections and heat stroke. In Mumbai, 2.5 million women do not even have a toilet in their homes and there are only free urinals for men in public. In the slums, there are only about six toilet rooms for 8000 women and even then women prefer to go somewhere outside. Sexual assaults often occur in public toilets, where women are first ambushed and then assaulted.

As hardly anyone wants to talk about this topic, there are no reliable figures for the number of sexual assaults that girls and women experience in public toilets. However, it is assumed that women experience sexual violence by men twice as often as women who have a toilet at home. However, relieving oneself outside increases the risk of diseases such as polio, pelvic inflammatory disease, hepatitis, cholera and worm infestation due to the lack of clean water. These diseases kill millions of people in India every year, mostly women and girls.

EDUCATION

Girls and women are also left behind when it comes to education. In developing countries, many of them do not go to school, and around two thirds of all illiterate women worldwide are women. One of the reasons for this is that many families cannot afford school fees. Even if school fees do not have to be paid, at least for primary school pupils, there are still costs for books, school uniforms and meals. Around 18% of all children between the ages of five and fourteen work, and this does not even include children who help with household chores.

Girls in particular have to help around the house; ten-year-old girls in Bangladesh spend an average of ten hours a day doing this. This means that, in addition to the financial aspect, there would also be no help in the household and patriarchal structures would be consolidated, so of several children only the boy is usually sent to school. Career opportunities are significantly better for boys anyway and the journey to school is often considered too dangerous for girls, whereas boys are expected to do the same.

Especially in crisis situations, such as wars or natural disasters, girls only go to school half as often as boys. Dependence on their future husbands is inevitable.

PROFESSIONAL LIFE

The gender pay gap is surveyed annually by the World Economic Forum and shows the difference in average gross income between the sexes. In terms of income, men and women are not yet on an equal footing, even if there are many reasons for this and it is not necessarily intentional. In fact, women earn less than men in every occupational group; in Germany, the pay gap is sometimes the largest. A distinction is made between the adjusted and unadjusted gender pay gap.

The adjusted gender pay gap is 2 - 7 % and takes into account comparable characteristics such as the same profession, the same qualifications and the same work experience. Despite having the same job and the same background, women in Germany therefore earn between 2 - 7 % less than men due to discrimination. Among other things, it is generally assumed that women will certainly become pregnant once and then be absent for a longer period of time, even though the birth rate continues to fall. However, it is directly assumed that a woman would not be able to reconcile work and family life, and this is used to justify cutting back on pay or not hiring in the first place.

The unadjusted gender pay gap is 18 %, which means that not only comparable characteristics are included in the calculation, but earnings as a whole. In other words, no account is taken of qualifications, occupation or work experience. Instead, the pay gap is largely due to the fact that women are more likely to work part-time due to the care work involved, which means they earn less and have few opportunities for promotion.

Due to possible pregnancies and maternity leave as well as parental leave, women are also absent for longer, which also has a negative impact on their careers. Another reason is that women are more likely to work in underpaid professions, particularly in the social sector, which are underpaid precisely because they are female-dominated. Men are more likely to work in prestigious and male-dominated professions such as the skilled trades, business and IT sectors, which are thus upgraded in monetary terms.

Despite equal demands and equal effort, female-dominated professions are considered by the general public to have lower salaries than male-dominated professions. Occupations in which women are heavily overrepresented include, for example, geriatric care and nursing or the profession of educator. These professions are comparatively poorly paid; in female-dominated fields (women make up 87% of nursing staff), they earn around €8 less per hour than in male-dominated professions. Nursing staff in particular bear enormous responsibility, have to perform physically demanding work, work in shifts, are exposed to high levels of psychological stress and have few opportunities to relax.

In addition, a refuse collector receives a bonus for lifting heavy loads, but a geriatric nurse does not. Even in professions that require an academic degree, you earn less in the female-dominated sector: a social worker earns around €16 per hour, an engineer around €29. One of the reasons for this difference is that the majority of typical female professions were never designed for a successful career. After all, women usually left the profession after the birth of their first child and took care of the upbringing and the household.

Although most people are in favor of better pay for traditional female professions, the actual situation is usually different. In a study, social researcher Katrin Auspurg found that, given the same qualifications and the same performance, the test subjects awarded the man a higher salary than the woman. As a result, most found a pay gap between the sexes of around 8 % despite equal work.

What also influences the gender pay gap is the different educational and career choices. This is influenced by gender stereotypes: certain sectors are seen as typically male or typically female, which means that women in particular are not confident in a male-dominated profession and consider themselves to be too untalented. Studies from 2001 and 2004 show that stereotypes such as the assumption that women cannot do mathematics, computer science or natural sciences influence their perception.

Despite their good performance, they do not feel able to perform as well as men in these subjects. Men, on the other hand, consider themselves more talented in these areas even if they perform equally well or worse than women. This goes so far that women make their further education and career path dependent on stereotypes and not on personal abilities. According to the TIMMS mathematics report and the TIMMS science report, girls are actually better at mathematics and science on average. But even with good grades, girls have little self-confidence in their abilities.

In addition, it is already difficult for women to enter the desired profession in the first place. According to a study by economists Dorothea Kübler, Robert Stüber and Julia Schmid, companies discriminate against women when hiring trainees, especially in male domains. Despite having the same qualifications and an equally good or even better degree, they are thought to be less likely to fit into the team and they want to avoid absenteeism due to potential pregnancies.

Another problem is that, particularly in small companies where only men have worked up to now, there are no sanitary facilities for women, which would therefore have to be built first. Many employers would rather save themselves the effort. According to the economists, the fact that an applicant is female has a similarly negative effect as a lower average grade by a whole grade.

A study conducted by Princeton University in 2012 also investigated the extent to which the gender of applicants influenced their chances of being hired and came to the same conclusion: the test subjects automatically assumed that a male applicant was more competent and would prefer to hire them. Only a gap of four years in the CV had a more negative effect than gender. Companies with a higher gender diversity were more successful:

Women often contribute characteristics that were previously less represented, such as better critical faculties, helpfulness, social interaction and they pay more attention to the suggestions of lower-ranking employees. In addition, more women in the company break down existing stereotypes. Hiring more women also helps to increase the proportion of women in the company in the future; having at least one woman in the application process increases the chances of female applicants. Men in female-dominated professions, on the other hand, hardly experience any discrimination.

Another point is the reluctance of women to negotiate salaries. This is mainly due to a lack of awareness of how much they can demand. According to economist and behavioral trainer Ljubow Chaikevitch, women in particular perceive themselves as being worth less than they actually are and are already grateful if they are hired at all. Especially if they enjoy their job, they tend to see it as a hobby and do not appreciate their own talents.

In fact, unlike men, women are brought up in childhood to be reserved, modest and quiet, and this rarely changes throughout their lives. For this reason, they tend to be punished for typically male behavior, which they are not used to and which manifests itself in self-confidence, dominance and a confident manner. Such behavior is not tolerated from them, as they are simply expected to be "nice" and modest. Men, on the other hand, are respected and even praised for the same behavior.

If you are in a position to want to negotiate a better salary yourself: Research your market value, the usual salary in your industry, talk to colleagues at the same hierarchical level and make a note of your successes at work. You should argue with your performance and added value, not with personal circumstances. It is also helpful to go through the salary negotiation meeting several times beforehand so that you can react calmly and confidently in the real meeting.

Motherhood is also a significant factor in the pay gap. As women take on the majority of care work and are less able to work full-time, let alone overtime, especially with children, they are at a disadvantage compared to their male colleagues. Thanks to their partner, men with children can usually work even more hours than before without children. What's more, women have a harder time in men's networks; going out for dinner or golf with colleagues or bosses after work is hardly possible with children at home.

For this reason, women are more likely to give up their desire for a steep career path; at the start of their career, around 43% of all women still want to be in management positions, but after five years in the job this figure drops to 16%. For men, the desire remains the same. According to a study by the German Institute for Economic Research (DIW Berlin), only one in four men take parental leave and most of them only take the two months that entitle them to parental allowance.

According to a study published in the American Journal of Sociology in 2007, mothers are also seen as less competent and less committed to their jobs than men and are paid less. Furthermore, mothers are expected to meet higher standards than men; they are less likely to be absent from work and must achieve better results. Surprisingly, it was found that this does not apply to fathers; lower demands are placed on them than on childless men.

Women face problems not only in terms of the application process, income or how they are perceived by others in their professional lives. They also have difficulties moving up the career ladder and reaching management positions. This is known as the "glass ceiling" effect.

Women usually come up against this obstacle from the middle management position onwards, above which they find it difficult to progress. The reason again lies in stereotypes that deny women their competence, qualifications and assertiveness, as well as in a male-oriented corporate climate and a lack of access to networks to make contacts. Studies have shown that men not only give priority to hiring men, but also to promoting them.

As in many other areas, it is also assumed that women will become pregnant and be absent for a longer period of time, so it is better to hire someone who does not run this risk. Women still experience discrimination and low esteem even when they have already climbed the career ladder. According to a survey from 2015, 75% of all female managers have already experienced discrimination. In 2012, the figure was only 61%.

They are discriminated against by not being treated as equals, being given company cars less often, being sent to fetch coffee more often or being made to perform similar menial tasks, as well as through sexist comments and insults. Discrimination also manifests itself in the fact that women are given worse projects, if they are considered at all in the selection process, are invited to networking events less often and receive lower salaries and bonuses. The male-oriented corporate culture also makes it difficult for women to realize their potential:

Women with children are restricted in their mobility, have at least small gaps in their CV and cannot be spontaneously available. However, this is normally expected. This problem would be solved if gender stereotypes were abandoned and men were encouraged to do more care work in order to free up women's time. Company kindergartens, working from home and flexible working hours also enable better performance.

Overall, however, it was refuted that women perform less well and cause a higher turnover rate. In addition, soft skills such as empathy, communication and organizational skills, active listening, critical thinking and motivation, which women in particular are trained to develop, are often underestimated. Although these qualities are appreciated at lower management positions, at higher levels it is typically male qualities such as assertiveness and determination that count most.

It has been found that women in senior management positions can significantly improve cooperation and ensure greater effectiveness and efficiency, as well as curb the excessive self-confidence of many CEOs. They are also better at crisis management and more open to suggestions and criticism. A gender-mixed group achieves greater success. Nevertheless, the proportion of women on the boards of a total of 2101 companies was only 7.7% in 2017. And 80.7% of companies have no women on their board at all. However, hardly any companies want to change the current situation: 78.2% of all companies have either no target or a target of zero for the proportion of women on the board.

In order to improve diversity in companies, a women's quota was therefore introduced in many places on January 1, 2016. In future, listed companies with more than three board members must have at least one woman on the board. Since the introduction of these requirements, the proportion of women in management positions at the companies concerned has risen from 25% to 35.4%. In the companies to which the regulations do not apply, it is only 19.9%.

In addition to the gender pay gap, there is also the gender pension gap, which shows the difference between the retirement incomes of men and women. Due to the reasons for the lower income described above, there is also a large difference here. With regard to the statutory pension alone, there is a gender pension gap of 58.5% in Germany. Men receive an average pension of €1,148, while women only receive a pension of €711. People affected by poverty in old age therefore often have to work part-time jobs or collect returnable bottles at an advanced age and can barely make ends meet. In addition, poverty in old age leads to a shortened life, health problems and social withdrawal.

HEALTH

In East Asia, South Asia, Central Asia and North Africa in particular, women are worth less than men; according to UNICEF, it is estimated that over one million fetuses are aborted every year in India and China alone simply because they are expected to be female.

Even as babies or small children, girls in these regions are often deliberately poorly cared for in order to bring about their death, or killed outright. In India, this is mainly for financial reasons; women are at a higher risk when they marry because of the dowry. In this dowry, goods or household goods are handed over from the bride's father to the groom's father, which means a high financial outlay. School and education costs are also high. In China, the abortion of female fetuses is more cultural, as women are generally considered to be of lesser value and the man is the head of the household.

In addition, the "one-child policy" was in force from 1978/1989 to 2015, during which a family was only allowed to have one child. Violations were punishable by a fine and sanctions such as losing one's job or home. Due to the Confucian tradition of maintaining male succession, girls were frequently aborted as a result.

According to a report by the United Nations Population Fund (UNFPA), poor girls and women have three times as many children as rich people due to a lack of access to contraception and education. Around 214 million women in developing countries are affected by a lack of access to contraception; 43% of all pregnancies are unintended. It is estimated that around 48 million children are aborted every year. According to German Development Minister Gerd Müller, primary education can reduce the pregnancy rate by 13% and secondary education by as much as 42%.

Contraceptives are seen as a means of freedom and self-determination, because since their introduction, women in Germany have been able for the first time to decide whether or not they want to expose themselves to the risk of pregnancy.

When the contraceptive pill came onto the market around 60 years ago, it was seen as a sign of emancipation. Over the years, the possible side effects became more and more noticeable; women suffered from mood swings, migraines, weight gain, loss of libido, poorer skin, panic attacks, depression, intermenstrual bleeding and an increased risk of thrombosis and cancer.

In a survey, a total of 55% of all women stated that contraception with the pill or other hormonal contraceptives such as the hormonal coil had negative effects on their body and mind. Young girls in particular are often not given sufficient information and are prescribed the pill, such as Tictacs, even though it has been proven to affect the body physically and psychologically.

When stopping the pill, the body sometimes needs six to twelve months to get used to the change, and many women only realize during this time how much they have changed under the influence of the pill. Given the extent of the side effects, the pill should no longer even be on the market from today's perspective.

The trend is now moving away from hormonal contraceptives towards condoms, the copper IUD, copper chain or measuring temperature and analyzing cervical mucus. Unfortunately, however, hardly any research is being carried out into non-hormonal alternatives, as hormonal contraceptives make a lot of money for the pharmaceutical industry. Contraception is still seen as a women's issue, for men there is only the condom, which is indirectly also used by women, and the vasectomy as a partially reversible cutting of the spermatic ducts. Although the male contraceptive pill is already on the market, 10% of test subjects complained of headaches, mood swings and loss of libido.

Although this occurred to the same extent as in women, the product was quickly discarded. If more intensive research were carried out into contraceptive options for men, they could relieve the burden on women and at the same time have a greater say in family planning. Even though alternatives are already being researched and the majority of men are in favor of more contraceptive options, there is still a lack of funding from the pharmaceutical industry. For the time being, contraception remains a women's issue.

It is not only the pill that is not being improved. There is a huge data gap in the field of medicine, as existing drugs are largely targeted at and researched on men. The male body is seen as the norm, the female body as "abnormal" and "atypical". It used to be assumed that the biology of men and women functioned more or less the same, but we now know better. Nevertheless, medicines are tailored to the typical 70-kilogram man, medical textbooks almost exclusively show male illustrations and gender-specific information is missing even on topics where gender differences have long been known. Such differences exist in particular for diseases such as depression, HIV, cancer, alcohol addiction and heart attacks.

A heart attack in a woman manifests itself through nausea, vomiting, back or neck pain and a feeling of tightness in the chest; in a man, on the other hand, through a stabbing pain in the chest that moves into the left arm. However, because medical schools primarily teach male symptoms, a heart attack in a woman is rarely if ever recognized. Clinical trials for drugs were presented as being valid for both men and women, even if only men were allowed to participate.

Side effects of medication in women are often not even listed in the package leaflet and the dosage of medication is usually intended for a man's body and has a completely different effect on a woman. These data gaps are known as the gender data gap. Since the 1990s, drug studies have also had to be carried out on women. Nevertheless, the proportion of female subjects in early phase I clinical trials is only 10 to 40 %, in phase II and III 30 to 80 %. In many areas, women would have had to participate twice as often in order to achieve sound results.

DESIGN

It's not just drugs that are aimed at men. When the safety of cars is to be tested, crash test dummies are used that are supposed to correspond to the human body. However, until recently, a dummy with a height of 1.77 meters and a weight of 76 kilograms was used for this purpose; in other words, a dummy that corresponds to the average male height. As a result, women have a 47% higher risk of being seriously injured and the risk of death is 17% higher.

As women are usually smaller and lighter, the headrest has a harder time absorbing the impact and the seat belt does not take breasts and a pregnant belly into account. And as women usually have to adjust the seat higher and further forward, they deviate from the standard position and thus increase the risk of internal injuries. An EU approval test now also requires the test to be carried out with a dummy adapted for women. However, this is only used on the front passenger seat and is only a smaller male dummy.

The male size, which should apply to all people, not only puts women at a disadvantage in the development of cars. Even pianos are tailored to fit an average man's hand, putting 87% of all adult female pianists at a disadvantage. This has an impact on their health, as they are more likely to suffer work-related illnesses and have twice the risk of pain. In addition, they can only perform on the piano with the same level of difficulty as men.

Another product that is designed for men's hands is the cell phone. An average-sized man can operate his smartphone normally, while an average-sized woman needs both hands. Google's voice recognition software was also programmed from a male perspective. As a result, the male voice is 70% more likely to be recognized than a woman's voice. This can even be dangerous: Voice recognition software in cars is supposed to increase driving safety and prevent distraction. But if there are problems because the software finds it more difficult to recognize a woman's voice, distraction is all the more likely.

The vice president of voice recognition at car navigation manufacturer ATX, Tom Schalk, said that women should simply adapt their voice to the system instead of the other way around. Blaming women for a problem they are not responsible for has always been easier than dealing with the root of the problem. In fact, women's voices are actually easier to understand because they speak more slowly and clearly and stretch the vowels more than men. Unfortunately, this doesn't help if the databases are only filled with male voices, on the basis of which software is then developed.

These are by no means all areas in which the design of a product is tailored to men. The office temperature is five degrees too cold for the average woman, doors are too heavy, furniture is too high. This list is not exhaustive, because many areas in which women are disadvantaged are not even known. The reason for this is that for centuries men were allowed to make all the decisions and only contributed their perspective; women were invisible in the background for a long time. Their bodies and their worldview have been treated as the universal norm and this is only slowly changing.

BODY POLITICS

Moreover, women are primarily judged in a derogatory way based on their appearance. Especially when they appear self-determined and self-confident, as is often the case with politicians, scientists or executives, their outfits are commented on or their bodies insulted.

The aim is to deny them their place, delegitimize them and show that they are not viewed with respect.

Overweight women are treated much less favorably than slim women. Appearance has always been important and attractive women have always been treated better and considered more likeable. However, today's proportions are unprecedented. Women are taught that they have to be beautiful to be valuable, which is questionable from a social, medical and moral point of view.

The media play a major role in disseminating the perfect body image of a woman and presenting it as the absolute ideal. In 5000 advertisements every day, women are told that they should please men and be a sex object. The cosmetics and fashion industry supports this, any blemishes on models' bodies are retouched and their bodies are photoshopped. Diet programs and protein shakes are more successful than ever. Female superheroes wear skimpy outfits and lots of make-up and the classic Barbie, who serves as a role model for many girls, would not even be viable due to her unrealistic body shape.

There are shows like "Germany's Next Topmodel", during which half of Germany makes fun of women's attempts at modeling. Flight attendants are required to wear certain make-up and high heels. And products or services related to appearance, such as razors and hairdresser visits, are more expensive for women than for men. Women are confronted everywhere with how they should look. Self-esteem is determined even more by the evaluation of their body than for men, because women have always been more the target of aesthetic representation than men. This leads to depression, cosmetic surgery and an increase in eating disorders.

VIOLENCE

What's more, women are affected by violence to an above-average extent; 81% of victims of domestic violence are women. Violence often takes place in close quarters, with a woman becoming a victim of assault by her partner every 45 minutes. According to an EU study, only one in three cases of domestic violence is reported. Sexual violence is the most common form of violence against women; 30% of all women in Europe are or have been victims. Of the 15 million girls aged 15 to 19 worldwide who have already experienced sexual violence, nine million have experienced it within the last year.

And surprisingly, in every fourth case, the perpetrator is the victim's own former or current partner. In cases of rape, sexual assault and sexual assault in a relationship, the woman is the victim in over 98% of cases, in 89% of cases of stalking, threats or assault, in 79.5% of cases of assault and in 76.4% of cases of homicide. Every day, a man tries to kill his current or previous partner, and every third day he succeeds. However, this is largely a taboo subject; the media often refer to it as a "family tragedy" or "jealousy drama". As a result, these so-called femicides are seen as isolated cases and not as a phenomenon affecting society as a whole. The emotional situation can even have a mitigating effect.

In fact, the violence experienced as a child has a significant impact on adult life. If you were abused by your parents, you are three times more likely to experience violence from your partner as an adult than children without such experiences. On top of this, 75% of all women have been sexually harassed at least once in their lives. The location of the harassment varies; it takes place on the internet, at home, at work, outside, during leisure time.

This does not only happen in socially disadvantaged groups or only in certain age groups, but equally everywhere. Harassment is perceived as humiliating and frightening. Victims of sexual assault often even have to justify themselves, as if they were in some way to blame. A sexual assault is often justified on the basis of the victim's clothing, as if one were challenging harassment and the perpetrator could not hold back if one was wearing a short dress. Clothing hardly plays a role here, as crimes against sexual self-determination do not decrease in winter when everyone is wearing warm clothes.

One cause of sexual assault is rather dominance and power behavior. The perpetrators want to dominate the other person and make them their own sexually. Another reason is the desire to act out sexual aggression towards a woman in order to take revenge on the entire female sex, who are allegedly responsible for all the misfortunes in the perpetrator's life. Most perpetrators have very low self-esteem, they have no respect and some are even sadistic.

The perpetrators of sexual harassment, which manifests itself in lewd comments, requests for sexual acts or the sending of sexist or pornographic photos, for example, also show similar traits. It is again about demonstrating power, degrading the other person and disrespect. For a long time, such crimes were not taken seriously, hushed up and dismissed as a trifle.

But a change is taking place: campaigns are being set up to raise awareness. Instead of "Protect your daughter", the message is now "Educate your son". There are more and more calls to report even supposedly minor harassment to the police to make it clear that such actions have consequences and are no longer accepted in silence. The MeToo debate in October 2017 went around the world. The hashtag #MeToo was used on social networks in the wake of the Harvey Weinstein scandal to draw attention to the scale of sexual harassment and sexual assault.

Harvey Weinstein, Hollywood's most influential film producer, had used his power to sexually harass, abuse, coerce or rape countless women. The women affected include his employees, colleagues and actresses such as Cara Delevingne, Angelina Jolie, Salma Hayek and Gwyneth Paltrow. After the two journalists Jodi Kantor and Megan Twohey from the New York Times reported on Weinstein's behavior, a chain reaction was triggered and more and more prominent women reported their experiences of sexual assault by Harvey Weinstein.

It became known that many people close to him, such as the entire board of the Weinstein Company and actor Ben Affleck, knew about this and yet kept the issue quiet. Subsequently, a public discussion about the deliberate ignoring of sexually aggressive behavior and harassment began and Harvey Weinstein was sentenced to 23 years in prison on March 11, 2020.

However, the hashtag MeToo was not only used in relation to Weinstein; fashion designer and producer Alyssa Milano called on Twitter for people to report their own experiences of sexual violence and harassment under #MeToo. The day after the call, the hashtag already had half a million tweets. In order to take tougher action against sexual harassment, the website "Dickstinction.com" was even set up, where you could easily report a "Dickpic" (a photo of a naked genital that someone has sent you). On top of this, there are discussions about including catcalling as a criminal offense in the penal code. Catcalling describes the lewd calling and whistling behind someone, is already a criminal offense in France and a few other countries and is only considered an insult in some cases in Germany.

LANGUAGE

The fact that men are considered the norm is still evident in language. When we talk about a mixed-gender group, we only use the masculine plural form: doctors, teachers, students and so on. This form is called the generic masculine. Generic means that the word is a universally valid generic term.

With this way of speaking, we use the man as the norm and make the woman invisible. Instead, they should simply feel that they are also meant. In reality, we realize that this is not the case. Girls and women do not feel addressed or meant by the masculine form. And it has already been established with schoolchildren that they only imagine male persons when a group uses the generic masculine form. Alternatively, gender-inclusive language is gaining ground, particularly in the media and at universities, where doctors, teachers, pupils, etc. are written with an asterisk after the word stem. This indicates both the masculine and feminine form and the asterisk in the middle indicates all other genders that are neither masculine nor feminine. Instead of the asterisk, a colon, the internal I, a slash or a gender-neutral formulation (e.g. "the teachers") can also be used for gendering in order to address non-binary persons.

Where the special character appears, a short gap is left when speaking. In this way, all genders are included and present. This has an effect: in a school class in which the gender was reversed, significantly more girls dared to take up male-dominated professions and deviate from the stereotypical role model. And when job advertisements were gendered, a significantly higher number of women applied. Although the generic masculine does not alone ensure that all genders are considered, it does have a supportive effect, as linguist Josef Klein found out. Critics find that gendering disrupts the flow of reading. However, studies have shown that it is possible to quickly become accustomed to the new way of writing and speaking if gender is used consistently.

IS FEMINISM ALSO FOR MEN?

As you can see, feminism is far from having reached its goal. Meanwhile, anti-feminism is on the rise worldwide; many men are afraid of impending changes and see their privileges threatened. In addition, feminism is often equated with hatred of men, although it merely criticizes the preferential treatment of men.

The increased presence of women often triggers a reluctance to engage in systematic misogynistic propaganda, particularly on the internet. Feminism is not just for women, it is against discrimination of all genders. Hardly any man would want a life characterized by power games, discrimination and oppression. After all, men also suffer from entrenched role clichés: it is hardly recognized by society that men show "moments of weakness". We are all familiar with sayings such as "be a man", "an Indian heart knows no pain" or insults such as "you girl" to criticize the expression of feelings, caring or tenderness.

The widespread image that men always have to be brave and strong is called toxic masculinity. As a result, men are less likely to seek help so as not to show their vulnerability. Many studies have shown that the stronger the adherence to classic masculinity norms, the higher the risk of developing depression. The proportion of registered mental illnesses is higher among women than men, but men commit suicide significantly more often. According to the Federal Statistical

Office, the proportion of male suicides in 2019 was around 76%.

The main cause of suicide is depression; over 70% of suicides had previously suffered from this illness. Even if men want to get help in time, depression is far less often recognized in them, as it is still considered a "women's disease" in the public consciousness. Because of this thinking, less research has been done on depression in men. It is now known that depression manifests itself differently in men than in women: Increased aggression and addictive behavior occur more frequently. Due to a lack of research and the resulting incorrect diagnoses, the number of unreported cases of depressed men is therefore significantly higher than previously assumed. It is not only in the area of mental illness that men seek help less often; they generally consult medical help less frequently and solve problems more often with violence, which leads to the frequent acts of violence against women described above.

Furthermore, according to a pilot study conducted by the Federal Ministry for Family Affairs, Senior Citizens, Women and Youth in 2004, men are more often victims of physical violence by other men; in 90% of all cases, the other party is male. As with domestic violence, this is often not taken seriously or hushed up, meaning that the exact number of incidents and victims is unclear.

Men also have a hard time as educators. There is not a single educator in over two thirds of all daycare centers; this is still a female-dominated profession. If a man decides to work as an educator, he attracts attention accordingly and is quickly placed under general suspicion of wanting to sexually abuse the children. Due to the traditional role model, many people find it unusual for a man to want to work with and educate children and accuse them of pedophilia without any evidence. In the past, men in education were therefore not even allowed to change children's nappies. This is despite the fact that male educators can demonstrably act as male role models for children, are just as professionally qualified as women and there is already a shortage of skilled workers in the sector. In order to improve social acceptance, advertising campaigns are now being run, lateral entry into the profession is being made possible and educators can network in online forums.

There are also disadvantages for men in relation to the school system. Girls tend to be rated better than boys, as they are often quieter, want to please the teachers and have nicer handwriting. Teachers are often unable to deal with pubescent pupils; puberty manifests itself differently in boys than in girls and is less understood. In addition, girls are better able to convince teachers to raise their grades because they tend to cry more often.

Even in family law, men experience discrimination more often than women. Until 2013, a father who was not married to the child's mother could not obtain custody against the mother's will. But this is not the only point in the law that discriminated against men until recently: regardless of the fact that compulsory military service is now controversial, until 2011 there was only a legal obligation for every male citizen to perform military service.

Since then, compulsory military service has been suspended, but not completely abolished. In the event of war, only men would have to do military service, women would not. This violates the principle of equal treatment in Article 3 of the Basic Law. Nevertheless, the Federal Constitutional Court ruled that compulsory military service was not invalid, as the legislator subsequently included "compulsory military service for men" in the law, thus creating a special law with priority over Article 3. However, this reasoning is questionable.

It is often argued that, on average, women are considered less suitable for military service than the average man due to physiological and biological differences. This is not convincing, as there are more than enough tasks in the Bundeswehr that can also be carried out by physically weaker people, and a gender-neutral criterion would have to be created.

After all, women can also be stronger than men, so a generalization seems nonsensical. Another popular argument is that women sacrifice a similar amount of their lives bearing and raising children or caring for relatives. This is also questionable, as women are not obliged to give birth, fewer and fewer children are being born anyway and men should be encouraged to take part in care work and parental leave. Nevertheless, the regulation is still characterized by the clichéd role model.

Studies show that men also fare better in a world of equal rights and equal status. Many men are already acting in a feminist way without realizing it. Perhaps you too have already supported feminism, for example by helping a woman who has been sexually harassed or by wanting to give a woman the same salary as male colleagues after her last job interview. Even if you have questioned common gender images, criticized your friends for sexist ideas or let your son play with dolls, you have already contributed to feminism. We achieve the most when we unite and fight together against injustice in the world, regardless of gender.

What can I do for feminism?

You have now learned what feminism is, what directions it takes, what it wants to achieve and why it is important. Unfortunately, according to the Ipsos Global Advisor study, only 28% of German women see themselves as feminist and only one in five men.

This puts Germany in fourth last place compared to 27 other countries. However, we should all see feminism as an opportunity to abolish gender-based discrimination in order to create a society without such differences. You can find out how to become a feminist in the following steps.

1. inform yourself!

Try to learn as much as you can about feminism and sexism and how they manifest themselves in our world and change it. You can read books on the subject, watch documentaries and reports or listen to podcasts and audio books. You can also ask your friends and acquaintances and talk about the topic. This will make you more aware of discrimination of all kinds and you can find out how you too are subconsciously influenced by internalized role models. This is the first step towards counteracting discrimination.

2. form your own opinion and defend it!

Once you have gathered enough information about feminism, you will be able to form an informed and objective opinion. Question your previous views and think for yourself, rather than accepting preconceived and popular views, and make your own decisions. Think about where you stand on a particular issue and discuss it.

Your opinion is important and deserves to be heard! Even if you can convince an acquaintance, a family member or a friend of the importance of feminism, you have already made a valuable contribution.

You can also become active and get involved politically or take part in demonstrations to express your opinion.

3. question yourself!

Questioning your own thoughts and behavior can be unpleasant and uncomfortable. You may find that you have unconsciously behaved in a sexist way. Perhaps you generally consider your opinion to be more important than that of women, often make derogatory comments about women, use sexist insults or tend towards mansplaining, where you generally assume that you know more about a topic than your female counterpart. However, insight is the first step towards improvement! If you have noticed that you have unconsciously internalized clichéd role models or discriminatory thought patterns, you can take action against this and do better in future.

4. identify yourself as feminist!

The term feminist still has negative connotations and is often equated with hatred of men. Show that it is not by identifying yourself as feminist. In this way, you normalize the term and help to remove the stigma. After all, all genders suffer from patriarchal structures, not just women.

5. show civil courage!

There are many situations in which you have to show courage and stand up for yourself or other people. Don't hesitate to step out of your comfort zone and take action against sexism. We all encounter it in everyday life, for example when men are told "Be a man!" and women are insulted as "bitches" for wearing short clothes.

Or when a woman is ordered to take minutes or fetch coffee, even though she has the same qualifications as her male colleagues. In addition, many women experience sexual harassment on a daily basis, whether at work, on the train or even among friends. Take action against this and show that you do not tolerate such behavior and that it should in no way be considered normal and acceptable. In this way, you can support everyone who is affected by it and encourage a rethink in your environment. After all, it's not about a battle between the sexes, but about the socially shaped image in society.

6. listen to those affected!

The best way to understand other perspectives is to listen to those affected who share their experiences of sexism. As an unaffected person, you will probably not even notice many things and will have a different mindset as a result. Based on other people's experiences, you can then develop your opinion and react more sensitively to discrimination.

7. engage with works by women!

Women are still underrepresented in the literature, music and film industries. Their works are perceived as less important and less valuable than those of men, without there being any evidence to support this. So look for books, films, works of art or pieces of music by women and engage with them. This will ensure that women become more present and visible in your thinking.

8 Encourage gender-neutral thought patterns in your children!

Children are shaped by social influences from an early age. Boys like blue, girls like pink. Boys like superheroes and play with cars, girls like princesses and play with dolls. Boys become doctors, girls become nurses. Boys can be loud and dominant, girls quiet and reserved. These are typical role models that are still internalized and promoted.

This way of thinking runs through the whole of life and is difficult to remove. It is also reflected in your behavior as an adult and can have considerable disadvantages. If you have children of your own, try to raise them in a gender-neutral way to counteract these disadvantages. Use your role model function! In this way, you will ensure that the entrenched gender roles are critically questioned and can promote the independent, self-determined development of your children.

www.ingramcontent.com/pod-product-compliance
Lightning Source LLC
Chambersburg PA
CBHW021745150726
47989CB00004B/1521